Stonehenge & Avebury

Henges are lonely and inspiring pagan temples that never occur outside the British Isles. Nearly 100 henges survive, scattered as far apart as Cornwall and the Orkney Isles. But, above all, it is in Wessex that henges are found, the four largest – Avebury, Durrington Walls, Marden and Mount Pleasant – as well as the most famous, Stonehenge.

A henge is a circular or oval area defined by a bank and a ditch and approached by one or two entrances. The bank is usually outside the ditch, so that the bank forms the boundary to a sacred area, separated physically and spiritually from the everyday world. Stonehenge itself is a curiosity on two counts: its bank is inside the ditch and within the henge stands the most elaborate set of prehistoric stones in Europe.

RIGHT: *Stonehenge, viewed from the fallen Slaughter Stone at the entrance.*

WHAT CAN BE SEEN TODAY?

The outer boundary of Stonehenge consists of a ditch, and a low bank that originally stood about 2m high. The boundary is interrupted by the broad entrance of the Avenue on the north-east side, and by several narrower entrances. Within the Avenue, near the road, stands the Heel Stone, and at the entrance to the site is the Slaughter Stone, now fallen, which formed part of a ceremonial doorway. Discs of white cement mark some of the 56 Aubrey Holes, arranged in a ring just inside the bank, and on this ring are two Station Stones, and two ditched enclosures that once contained similar stones.

The outer circle of standing stones is known as the Sarsen Circle. This consisted of a ring of 30 uprights crowned by a continuous ring of 30 lintels. Within this ring is the incomplete Bluestone Circle, originally consisting of about 60 stones. The Sarsen Trilithons inside these circles originally numbered five and formed a horseshoe shape, and within this stood the Bluestone Horseshoe, originally of 19 stones that increased in height toward the centre. At the very heart is the Altar Stone, now buried in the ground beneath fallen stones.

LEFT: *This aerial view shows the central stones surrounded by the earlier bank and ditch. The Slaughter Stone, the leaning Heel Stone and the banks at the start of the Avenue can be seen near the road.*

Visitors always want to know when Stonehenge was built, but only recently have we been able to give the right answer. John Aubrey, in the 17th century, ascribed it to the 'ancient Britons' who lived here before the Roman invasion of AD 43; others attributed it to the Danes who followed the Romans; William Stukeley, in the 18th century, got carried away by his false Druidic fantasies and so started a misconception still current today. The first to establish the correct period was Professor William Gowland who, in 1901, excavated the base of a leaning stone so carefully that he was able to conclude that Stonehenge had been constructed 'during the period of transition from stone to bronze'.

When Stonehenge passed into public ownership in 1918, the Society of Antiquaries supported a long campaign of excavations by Colonel William Hawley from 1919 to 1926. In many ways this was a disaster, because Hawley's patient but unthinking digging, only described in the briefest of published summaries, has damaged the evidence forever. The involvement of Professor Richard Atkinson from the late 1940s began with an attempt to recover the information lost by Hawley's endeavours and ended in triumph in 1963, with the whole sequence of construction clearly understood. Far from being built at one time, drastic remodelling of the monument had continued over some 1,700 years, straddling very broadly the 'transition from stone to bronze'. Atkinson divided the sequence into four main phases (see plans on p.5).

Phase I

In this phase, corresponding to about 2800 BC, a rather modest henge about 91m across was dug, with a standard north-east entrance. For a Wessex henge, however, it already had unusual features: the bank inside the ditch, instead of the other way around, and a circle of 56 Aubrey Holes, small, steep-sided, round pits dug just inside the bank. This date falls in the middle of the British neolithic period and the characteristic finds here are fragments of pottery known to specialists as 'Grooved Ware' from their style of decoration. During Phase I the Heel Stone, which weighs about 35 tonnes, and its companion were erected like a gun-sight just beyond the entrance to the henge.

Phase I may have ended with a time of abandonment: snails called 'Zonitidae' became abundant, indicating that ungrazed grassland took over the site. In the surrounding plain, tracts of formerly agricultural land became a wilderness. Perhaps the henge continued to be used in a state of partial dereliction merely as an enclosed cemetery. Hawley found about 30 cremation burials from the later neolithic period, cut into the chalk filling of the Aubrey Holes.

LEFT: *The Heel Stone, originally upright, is the only megalith to survive outside the ditch of the henge. It is a large unworked sarsen and the nearest source would have been the Marlborough Downs east of Avebury, a journey of some 36km. Originally a pair of Heel Stones flanked the line to the midsummer sunrise.*

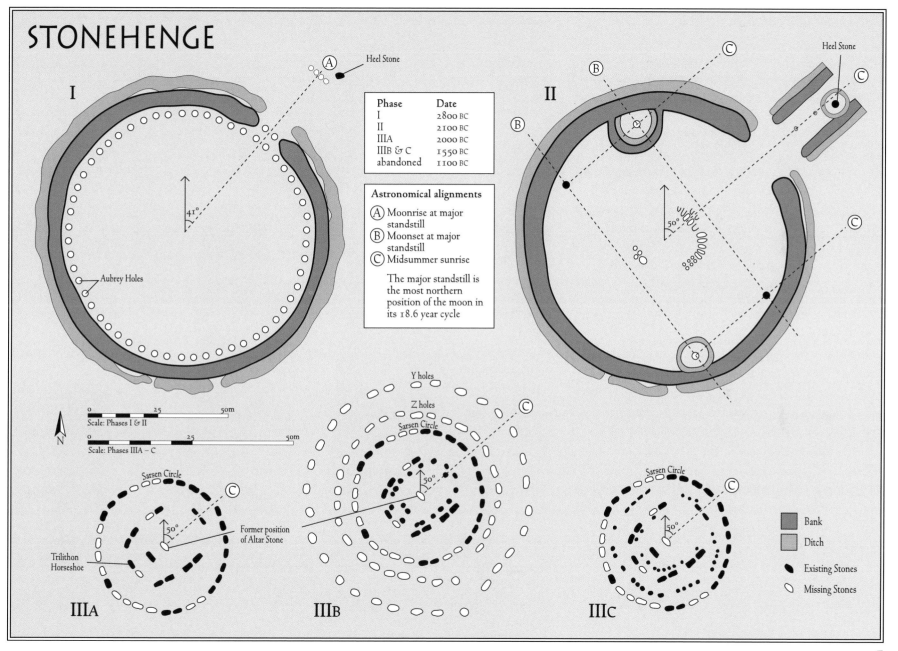

STONEHENGE

I

Heel Stone

Aubrey Holes

41°

Phase	Date
I	2800 BC
II	2100 BC
IIIA	2000 BC
IIIB & C	1550 BC
abandoned	1100 BC

Astronomical alignments

Ⓐ Moonrise at major standstill

Ⓑ Moonset at major standstill

Ⓒ Midsummer sunrise

The major standstill is the most northern position of the moon in its 18.6 year cycle

II

Heel Stone

50°

0   25   50m
Scale: Phases I & II

0   25   50m
Scale: Phases IIIA – C

N

Y holes

Z holes

Sarsen Circle

Sarsen Circle

50°

IIIA

Former position of Altar Stone

50°

Trilithon Horseshoe

IIIB

50°

Sarsen Circle

IIIC

50°

Bank

Ditch

Existing Stones

Missing Stones

Phase II

In c.2100 BC there were developments by the 'Beaker' people, so called from the characteristic shape of their pottery. Their arrival marks the earliest phase of the Wessex Bronze Age. A new north-easterly alignment was emphasised by the Avenue, a broad embankment extending 510m outside the ditch and still visible today. The entrance to the henge had to be widened by throwing down part of the bank to make it symmetrical with this slightly different axis. The four Station Stones were placed in a huge rectangle which has an undoubted astronomical significance (see pp.5 and 13). At the same time, the mysterious bluestones were introduced as two modest circles in the centre of the henge, each with an entrance looking straight along the Avenue.

RIGHT: *A curved lintel of the Sarsen Circle, showing a tongued joint to locate the groove of a missing lintel.*

STONEHENGE

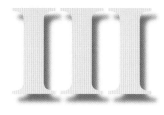

Phase III

It was Phase III that made Stonehenge such a remarkable monument. Professor Atkinson discerned three separate episodes of remodelling. The first, known as IIIA and dated c.2000 BC, was the most spectacular and is the part that everybody remembers – the giant Trilithon Horseshoe and the Sarsen Circle around it. The sarsens – natural sandstone blocks found on the Marlborough Downs to the north of Stonehenge – were worked to a precise shape with stone hammers. The geometry of the continuous lintel is truly amazing: it is accurately circular and precisely level despite the sloping site. Each component is cut to form a circular arc, linked to its neighbour by a vertical tongue-and-groove joint and held on its upright by a mortice-and-tenon joint. This daring and unique monument corresponds to far-reaching changes in society. The Bronze Age was not simply a time of advancing technology: society underwent profound changes, particularly with the strong development of a hierarchy. Status became supremely important and this is reflected in the magnificent style of the Stonehenge burials.

Stonehenge is surrounded by scores of prominent round barrows where the chieftains and their queens were interred, for the first time in Britain, with valuable weapons and elaborate ornaments.

Phase IIIB followed in c.1550 BC, when the Y and Z holes were dug in concentric circles outside the settings of sarsens, and the bluestones were re-erected in an oval arrangement within the horseshoe. For some reason the bluestones were moved again quite soon – Phase IIIC is also dated c.1550 BC – this time to the present setting of an oval between the Trilithon Horseshoe and the Sarsen Circle, plus a second horseshoe nestling within the large one.

RIGHT: *The surviving upright of the central trilithon, the tallest stone at Stonehenge. The tenon on top would have formed a joint with a mortise in the lintel.*

STONEHENGE

IV

Phase IV

In this phase, dated c.1100 BC, the Avenue, already 1,000 years old, was extended by two straight stretches for a further 2km, which brought it down to meet the River Avon. The project, however, was abandoned before the ditches were completed and this newer section can no longer be seen, except from the air as a crop mark. Associated with this phase is a style of pottery ascribed by archaeologists to the 'Deverel-Rimbury' people, intensive farmers who introduced the ox-drawn plough. Their arrival coincided with a great change in customs and beliefs. The old gods, perhaps, had proved false. They and their temple were abandoned, this time forever.

LEFT: *This is the best-preserved part of the Sarsen Circle. The entrance was beneath the middle of the three lintels. The lintels are curved and the uprights upwardly tapered.*

WHY IS STONEHENGE IN RUINS?

Only a quarter of the Sarsen Circle remains intact and what survives of the Trilithon Horseshoe has been largely re-erected. Yet it may be wrong to assume that this damage was caused by natural forces. After all, the method of construction of the Sarsen Circle was very sound, with all the stones locked together by 'woodwork' joints and the uprights socketed firmly in packed chalk. Solitary megaliths all over Britain stay upright, so there is no reason why Stonehenge should fall down, even after 4,000 years. A viable hypothesis is that some unknown Roman general deliberately slighted the monument, mistakenly believing that it was a stronghold of the Druids, their fiercely independent opponents, whom the Romans condemned for practising human sacrifice.

LEFT: *Many of the sarsens and bluestones at Stonehenge are now leaning, fallen, broken or missing.*

THE MYSTERY OF THE BLUESTONES

The origin of the Stonehenge bluestones is highly evocative. Twenty-nine of the blocks are dolerite, a beautiful intrusive rock with highly unusual white or pink spots of albite-oligoclase felspar. Four more are rhyolite, a compact, light blue-grey volcanic rock, often conspicuously banded.

As long ago as 1858, Sir Andrew Ramsay noted the bluestones' similarity to the Lower Silurian igneous rocks of north Pembrokeshire. Then, in 1923, Herbert Thomas, a petrographer with the Geological Survey, astounded the Society of Antiquaries with his proof of the actual source of the bluestones. He found outcrops of both the dolerite and the rhyolite, 'identical in the minutest detail' with his Stonehenge samples, on the Mynydd Preseli (Prescelly Mountains) of north Pembrokeshire. The occurrence of the outcrops of these highly individual rocks so close together is extremely suggestive of some special religious value or healing property having been attached to these particular stones and no others. The eastern Mynydd Preseli are themselves very rich in megalithic monuments – the remains of seven stone circles may still be found there today. Conceivably, the bluestones were originally erected on Mynydd Preseli and transported, some 4,500 years ago, as an already venerated stone circle, to Stonehenge.

RIGHT: This grooved bluestone from the Bluestone Horseshoe was formerly jointed to another with a corresponding ridge.

HOW WERE THE BLUESTONES MOVED?

Herbert Thomas favoured a totally overland journey of about 290km but, by not specifying its course, he did not have the difficult task of defending his route in detail!

Widely preferred today is the following land and water route of about 360km: (1) overland for about 15km from the outcrops to the navigable point of the Eastern Cleddau; (2) about 40km down the Eastern Cleddau; (3) about 185km up the Bristol Channel from Milford Haven to Avonmouth; (4) about 50km up the Somerset Avon; (5) about 20km overland from Trowbridge to Heytesbury; (6) about 25km down the river Wylye; (7) about 20km up the Wiltshire Avon; and (8) about 3km along the Stonehenge Avenue.

STONEHENGE

The most complete part of the outer circle of sarsens, spanning the entrance, with stones of the Bluestone Circle inside it.

THE ASTRONOMER-PRIEST THEORY

The late Professor Alexander Thom, although an engineer, spent much of his life trying to demonstrate that stone circles and rows were built to study solar and lunar astronomy. So well did megalithic man know the movements of the heavens, claimed Thom, that he could predict which full or new moon would give rise to an eclipse of the moon or of the sun. Observations were made when objects rose or set and these points on the horizon were marked, according to the astronomical theory, either by stone alignments or by distant foresights, such as mounds or notches on the skyline. Thom surveyed Stonehenge and found no distant markers, concluding that here was an astronomical temple more for ceremony than for accurate observation.

RIGHT: *Looking through the Sarsen Circle towards the Heel Stone at the entrance, at sunrise.*

Although many prominent archaeologists in the 1960s and 1970s challenged it, this theory has, broadly speaking, stood the test of time. The latest research has shown that Stonehenge began as a lunar temple, but was later modified for worship of the sun. The four Station Stones, arranged during Phase II in a huge rectangle, indicate, with their long sides, the moon setting in its extreme north position. At the same time the rectangle's short sides indicate the midsummer sunrise. Only at, or close to, the latitude of Stonehenge will a rectangle fulfil this dual function. The original entrance from Phase I of the henge aligned with the most northerly rising of the moon, the 'major standstill'. Fifty-three stake holes in six arcs have been found across the entrance to the henge. They were used during the century of observation which was required to define the bearing of 41°. This preoccupation with the moon is probably connected with rituals of death. But quite soon the astronomer-priests changed their entrance to a bearing 9° further south, thus aligning the henge with the midsummer sunrise. As the priest performed his solstice rites at dawn in the exact centre of the temple he would see the sun rise exactly between the Heel Stone and its companion.

Modern-day druids and other interested visitors celebrate the summer solstice at the temple of Stonehenge.

STONEHENGE

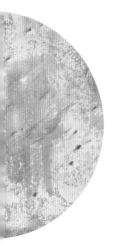

Stonehenge, of course, did not arise in splendid isolation. The modern visitor who stands and looks out onto Salisbury Plain can still see and explore monuments of the rich ritual landscape. Most obvious of all are the burial mounds of the Bronze Age elite. The nearest such round barrow is a mere 60m outside the henge. But cemeteries can be seen, sited on prominent ridges, in all directions: on the eastern horizon cluster the King Barrows, to the north-west the Cursus Barrows and, across the dry valley to the south, the Normanton Down Barrows. Many more lie hidden, but all the Bronze Age types are there for the visitor to find in a morning's walk.

Over a dozen long barrows in the area precede Stonehenge, dating from c.3700 to 3000 BC. Archaeologists, who used to see them as just tombs, now recognise long barrows as territorial markers and the first temples. The best example is the founder member of the Winterbourne Stoke cemetery (see map on p.33).

Neolithic ideas on the disposal of the dead seem distinctly grisly today. People then believed that the spirit lingered in the corpse until all the flesh had been stripped from the bones. Only then could the bones be safely buried. Corpses had to be exposed for about two years to decay naturally. To prevent the bodies being ripped apart by scavengers, special mortuary houses were built. This is a favoured explanation for the elaborate post-holes found at nearby Woodhenge. Possibly Phase I of Stonehenge itself included a central wooden mortuary house.

The Cursus, a fine neolithic monument, also pre-dates Stonehenge. As its true purpose still remains obscure, experts see it simply as 'ceremonial'. Death and its rituals, perhaps funeral processions or games, were somehow involved, judging from the way a long barrow formed its eastern terminus and round barrows cluster close by. The Cursus lies just 800m north of Stonehenge and extends for 2.7km, from the present Fargo Plantation, across a shallow dry valley, into the Larkhill Barracks. A visit to the Cursus itself, and the Cursus Barrows, forms a most rewarding short walk.

LEFT: *A group of round barrows called the King Barrows can be seen in beech woods to the east of Stonehenge.*

Spring snow casts a mysterious stillness over Britain's most important prehistoric monument.

The awe-inspiring sight of Stonehenge sharply silhouetted against a dramatic sunset.

STONEHENGE

Sunrise at Avebury.

THE STONEHENGE AND AVEBURY PEOPLE

Sunrise at Avebury, with the Barber Stone in the foreground, and sarsens of the Southern Circle behind.

Who were the Stonehenge and Avebury people and how did they live? The early Wessex farmers chose the dry chalk uplands because it was easy to clear the forests with their polished stone axes and work the light soil with their simple wooden ploughs or 'ards'. We know what they ate from the remains of numerous feasts, such as those found in the Coneybury pit about 1km from Stonehenge – bones of cattle and roe deer, with some red deer, pig, beaver and fish. Elsewhere there is evidence of sheep, always a success on cleared downland, and goats. The area's soil has now been cultivated for over 5,000 years and has lost most of its humus and loess content. In neolithic times it would have been much more fertile, producing such nutritious crops as pulses and beans. Actual plant remains and textile fragments from the Bronze Age have been found preserved in a unique location in the Stonehenge area: the damp conditions at the bottom of a 30m-deep well known as the Wilsford Shaft.

Using new techniques, we now know the broad effects on the environment of the prehistoric activities. Most of the earliest Wessex farming was pastoral, with cultivation restricted to small plots. In early neolithic times the forest clearings around Stonehenge expanded rapidly to exploit the rich soil. But by the later neolithic period the dwindling woodlands needed careful management. By the early Bronze Age, sheep grazed large areas of established pasture. In fact the tree cover became so sparse that the landscape of 2000 BC was beginning to assume the open appearance of today.

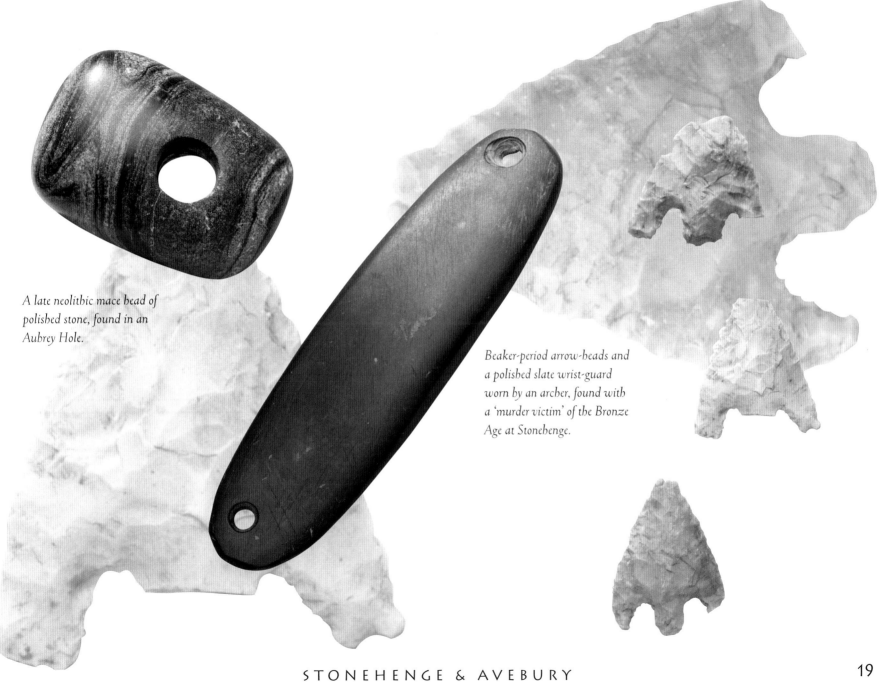

A late neolithic mace head of polished stone, found in an Aubrey Hole.

Beaker-period arrow-heads and a polished slate wrist-guard worn by an archer, found with a 'murder victim' of the Bronze Age at Stonehenge.

RIGHT: *An avenue of standing stones, the West Kennet Avenue connected Avebury to the Sanctuary on Overton Hill.*

As a result of the Roman propaganda against the Celtic Druids, human sacrifice in prehistoric Britain has often been taken for granted. Now the excavators have provided proof. In the open space at the centre of Woodhenge, an interesting site with open access 3km north-east of Stonehenge, was found the shallow grave of a $3^{1}/_{2}$-year-old girl, facing the entrance and the rising sun, her skull neatly split in two by an axe. Another foundation sacrifice turned up at Avebury's Sanctuary: the body of an adolescent youth, aged 14 years, emphasised an important barrow alignment when the temple was last rebuilt. Perhaps we condemn these practices too easily. 'Human sacrifice should not be equated with our modern attitude to murder', says Aubrey Burl in *Rites of the Gods*. 'It symbolised some need in society, whose urgency and necessity was more keenly stated if the chosen symbol was a human being.'

Another famous death is the 'Stonehenge murder': in 1978 the body of a tall strong man, aged about 27 years and dating from the earlier Bronze Age, was found in the ditch of the henge. There were three arrow-heads with the corpse, the tips of two of which were found lodged in his rib cage. The victim had been shot from close range and then thrown into a hastily dug pit with the arrow-shafts still protruding from his body. When found he was still wearing his slate wrist-guard and so was presumably an archer himself.

LEFT: *Carved on the inner side of a trilithon are a dagger and an axe-head.*

The Stonehenge environs have now yielded many ceremonial symbols to intrigue us. A chieftain buried under the Bush Barrow, for example, took with him to the other world the symbols of his earthly power – a mace-head of rare limestone, its shaft enriched by bone mounts, a bronze axe, and three copper and bronze daggers, one with a handle inlaid with thousands of minute gold pins – not to mention his earthly wealth expressed by hammered-gold belt ornaments. Maceheads and ceremonial axes of semi-precious stone, such as jadeite, played a central role in the priests' authority and rites. Buried in the Aubrey Holes of the early henge were chalk balls and flint rods, understood by Burl to be phallic symbols, and cups, which may be symbols of female sexuality.

The Avebury temple seems to have been strongly connected with the great human themes of fertility, life and death. Rich evidence of funerary feasts has been found at the Sanctuary, which was linked by a procession route, the West Kennet Avenue, to the henge. The columnar and triangular stones of this avenue were deliberately paired together. Such a strong sexual symbolism implies a close connection between fertility and funerary rites. This celebration of the cycle of birth, life and death was a central part of neolithic philosophy.

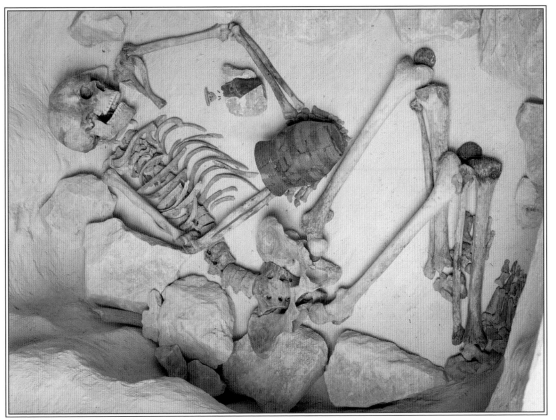

LEFT: *A Beaker burial from a barrow at Shrewton, dating from around 2000 BC, with a pot and a bronze knife.*

AVEBURY

In the 17th century, the antiquarian, John Aubrey, noted that Avebury far surpassed Stonehenge 'as a Cathedral doth a Parish Church'. Sir Richard Colt Hoare was also much impressed and wrote, in *Ancient Wiltshire* (1812): 'With awe and diffidence I enter the sacred precincts of this once hallowed sanctuary, the supposed parent of Stonehenge, the wonder of Britain and the most ancient, as well as the most interesting relict which our island can produce.' Of the four Wessex 'superhenges' that are more than 300m across, Avebury's earthworks are by far the most impressive today. They also contain some of the largest megaliths in Britain and the great stone circle is the largest of its kind in Europe. The area has been inhabited by villagers for about 1,000 years, and so it comes as a surprise to learn that it remained unknown to outsiders until Aubrey rode through the village on a hunting trip in 1648.

RIGHT: *This aerial view shows the vast area of the Avebury henge. The four original entrances in the prehistoric earthwork are still used today.*

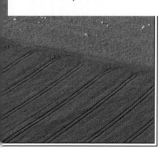

WHAT CAN BE SEEN TODAY?

The outer boundary of Avebury is formed by a tall bank and a deep ditch. Four modern roads enter the henge through the original gaps in the bank and causeways across the ditch: the West Kennet Avenue still leads into the south entrance. Immediately within the inner lip of the ditch, and keeping a constant distance from it, is the Great Circle, an irregular ring of stones that originally consisted of about 98 sarsens. Inside the Great Circle are two separate, equal-sized, exactly round circles. The Southern Circle was originally formed of 29 stones. At its centre is a plinth that marks the site of an obelisk that once stood there. This plinth also forms the centre of a partly surviving D-shaped setting of small rough sarsens, called the Z feature. The Northern Circle consisted of two concentric rings, the outer having 27 stones and the inner 12 stones. At its centre are two of the three sarsens that once formed a rectangular cove. Much of the village of Avebury stands within the temple.

LEFT: *The huge sarsens of Avebury's Southern Circle.*

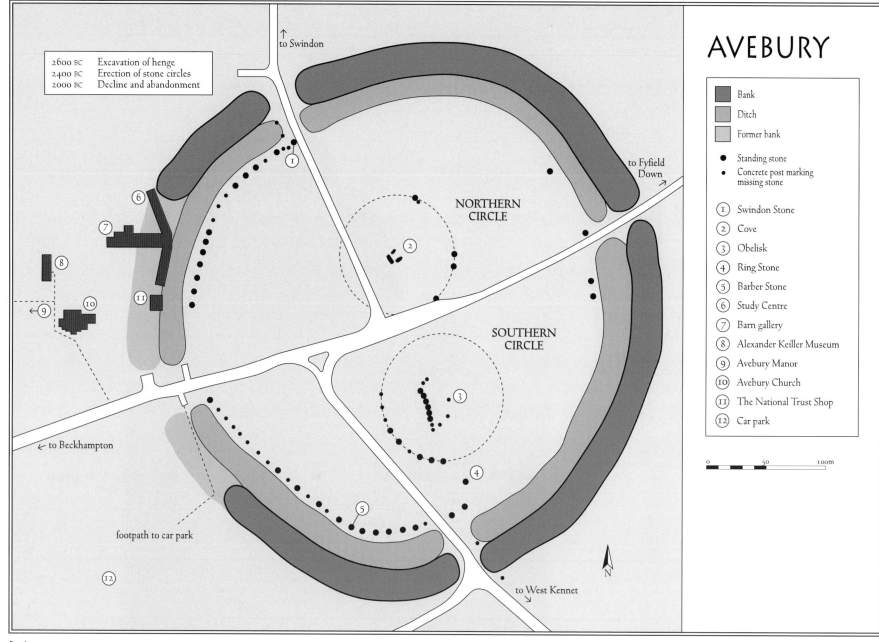

AVEBURY

2600 BC	Excavation of henge
2400 BC	Erection of stone circles
2000 BC	Decline and abandonment

to Swindon

to Fyfield Down

NORTHERN CIRCLE

SOUTHERN CIRCLE

to Beckhampton

footpath to car park

to West Kennet

N

Bank

Ditch

Former bank

● Standing stone

• Concrete post marking missing stone

① Swindon Stone
② Cove
③ Obelisk
④ Ring Stone
⑤ Barber Stone
⑥ Study Centre
⑦ Barn gallery
⑧ Alexander Keiller Museum
⑨ Avebury Manor
⑩ Avebury Church
⑪ The National Trust Shop
⑫ Car park

0   50   100m

CONSTRUCTION OF THE GREAT HENGE

LEFT: *Avebury's bank was originally separated from the ditch by a broad platform, and its inner edge was retained in places by a low wall of chalk blocks.*

After digging at Windmill Hill, a mid-neolithic site about 2km north-west of Avebury, Alexander Keiller bought Avebury and carried out a campaign of exemplary excavations through the 1930s. His team revealed how far the ditch has filled up since it was dug. When looking into the ditch today, visitors need to realise that it was first dug out no less than 6m below the present turf. Imagine the bank perhaps 5m higher than it is today, faced on the inside with a wall and gleaming white with fresh chalk, and you have some idea of its original appearance.

BELOW: *Sarsens of the Southern Circle, at dawn.*

In c.2600 BC, or about 2,000 years after the first farmers reached Wessex, the building of Avebury began. They chose a lowland plain at the foot of the Marlborough Downs. Like most henges, the site is close to water, in this case the infant River Kennet. Using antlers as picks, the shoulder blades of cattle as shovels, and woven baskets, gangs dug out the ditch and threw up the bank outside. The precise shape was not important. It would have been simple to define an exact circle with a rope stretched tight from the centre, but it seems that the priests who first marked out the sacred enclosure were quite content to pace out a shapeless ring (see photo on p.22 and plan on p.24). If geometry was insignificant at this stage, the tremendous scale of the excavation was clearly vital. About 120,000 cubic metres of solid chalk were dug from the ditch at Avebury, a volume about 60 times greater than the spoil from the ditch at Stonehenge. Only one earthwork can compare in size to Avebury: the 250,000 cubic metres of chalk and soil excavated to form Silbury Hill, just 1.5km to the south of Avebury. The two biggest neolithic earthworks in Europe somehow form part of the same ritual landscape.

THE STONE CIRCLES

It has been estimated that there was originally a minimum of 247 standing stones within the henge and perhaps 400 more forming the two avenues outside. The heaviest remaining megalith, the Swindon Stone near the north entrance, weighs about 65 tonnes, but the survivors average about 15 tonnes. The Avebury stones are sarsens of the same geological type as those of Stonehenge. At Avebury, the sarsens were selected for their shape and used in their natural state, whereas at Stonehenge they were laboriously worked to a precise geometry. The Avebury builders preferred their stones to be either columnar or flat with a square or triangular outline.

The transport and erection of these stones in about 2400 BC represent one of the great triumphs of prehistoric building. Experts agree that they once lay on the surface of the surrounding hills and valleys, especially the Marlborough Downs. Neolithic and more modern builders have since removed all the natural boulders from the immediate surroundings but, if you follow Green Street out of the henge to the east, a chalk track will take you 3km to the main source area. There, on Fyfield Down, natural sarsens still litter the lonely sheepwalks, although the heaviest ones were taken away some 4,000 years ago.

The builders chose to raise three sacred circles inside their temple. Despite their popular name, prehistoric stone circles are rarely circular. This is certainly true of the Great Circle, which follows the irregular plan of the henge, keeping a constant distance from the inner lip of the ditch. Originally it must have consisted of about 98 stones, but their partial destruction means that we can no longer tell whether the columnar and triangular shapes were placed at random or in some meaningful pattern. The huge size of the Great Circle

ABOVE: *The Swindon Stone, at the west of the north entrance, is the largest megalith at the temple of Avebury.*

AVEBURY

allows ample space within it for the two separate, exactly round circles that contain very different ritual features. The centre of the Southern Circle was emphasised by a 6.4m tall obelisk. Stukeley drew it lying on the ground in 1723, but all that was left for Keiller to record in the 1930s was the large burning pit used to break it up. A similar fate befell most of the stones that were once equally spaced around the Southern Circle. It is rare for any feature to mark the centre of a stone circle, and this obelisk is made more unusual by forming the centre of a mysterious D-shaped setting of small rough sarsens, the so-called Z feature, which partly survives. The Northern Circle is just as fragmentary, and at its centre two stones remain of a rectangular cove known as the 'Devil's Brandirons'. Originally a setting of three sarsens, this probably imitated the burial stall of a megalithic chambered tomb. But instead of being hidden under the dark earth of a barrow, the Avebury cove was a giant niche open to the sky, the setting for some public ritual of death.

ABOVE: *The north-west quarter of Avebury's Great Circle, with the 65-tonne Swindon Stone in the foreground.*

The two surviving stones of the cove,
at the centre of the Northern Circle,
with one of the circle's stones beyond.

HOW WERE THE STONES MOVED AND ERECTED?

A knowledge of the available technology makes wooden rollers the most likely method of transport, with the exact route carefully chosen to avoid steep and dangerous gradients. Once at their site, a small socket, only about 1m deep, was dug into the chalk and lined with wooden stakes that would help to guide the foot of the stone into the correct position. Ropes, wooden props and levers gradually raised the stone to the vertical in its socket. This was a laborious process – an experiment by Alexander Keiller's team in 1934 showed that 14 untrained men would take four days to erect one small flat stone using neolithic methods. Great care was taken to place the centre of gravity directly over the middle of the hole. The final act was to ram a hard packing of chalk, flints and small sarsens around the base of the megalith to hold it firmly in its socket. The stability achieved is particularly impressive in the case of the giant Swindon Stone, which has spent 4,000 years balanced on one corner with only a fragment of its bulk underground.

The Avebury temple remained in active use for about 700 years. Towards the end of this period, c.2000 BC, the 75 Stonehenge sarsens were collected from the rich source on the Marlborough Downs. The difficulty of fording the River Kennet further downstream raised the fascinating possibility that these sarsens were a gift from the Avebury people and passed through their completed temple for the priests to sanctify them. Rodney Castleden believes it likely that the Beckhampton Avenue, which left from the west of the henge, was actually built to celebrate the first part of their long and ponderous journey to Stonehenge.

BELOW: A house in the village of Avebury provides an attractive backdrop to stones of the Northern Circle.

RIGHT: *The Barber Stone killed a travelling barber-surgeon who was helping to overthrow it early in the 14th century.*

The ceremonial landscape around Avebury is perhaps even richer than the Stonehenge environs. The main elements are: the stone-chambered West Kennet Long Barrow, (in use from 3700 to 2200 BC); the unchambered Beckhampton Road Long Barrow (3250 BC); the large causewayed camp on Windmill Hill (3300 BC); the Sanctuary, a temple on Overton Hill (three phases, from 3000 to 2500 BC); the gigantic Silbury Hill mound (three phases, from 2700 to 2500 BC); the double avenues of standing stones to the Sanctuary and Beckhampton (2400 BC); and finally the numerous round barrows on the surrounding ridges (c.1800 BC).

Over the last 1,000 years, many of the standing stones in this landscape have been destroyed, some broken up with fire and water, others toppled and buried. One culprit, a medieval barber-surgeon, died in the act of destruction, crushed under a falling megalith at Avebury in about 1325 – we can date his death from the coins found in his purse.

RIGHT: *Part of the interior of the stone-chambered West Kennet Long Barrow, in which some 42 people were buried.*

WEST KENNET LONG BARROW

This magnificent stone-chambered long barrow dates from c.3700 BC and at about 107m in length is the largest long barrow in England. It is constructed of large sarsens and drystone walling, with huge capstones forming the roof. The tomb was once sealed with the sarsens and flanking stones that now obscure the entrance.

SILBURY HILL

An earthwork even larger than Avebury, Silbury Hill excites our wonder as a neolithic engineering triumph: its complex network of internal retaining walls still prevents the rubble-fill from slumping. It superficially resembles a gigantic Bronze Age barrow, but we now know it was built 1,000 years earlier and contains no burials. Was it a harvest hill, symbolising the earth-goddess pregnant with each year's new crops?

RIGHT: *The mysterious Silbury Hill's enormous size (325,000 cubic metres) is a central feature of Avebury's landscape.*

GLOSSARY

AVENUE
A processional or ritual way, usually marked out by two parallel banks.

BEAKERS
Characteristic pottery (c.2500–1900 BC) of neolithic invaders known as 'Beaker' people.

BRONZE AGE
Period of bronze technology, beginning in Britain c.2000 BC.

CAUSEWAYED CAMP
Mid-neolithic hilltop settlement surrounded by irregular banks and ditches.

CURSUS
Mid-neolithic linear earthwork with parallel banks and unknown ritual purpose, up to 9.6km long.

DEVEREL-RIMBURY
A mid-Bronze Age culture.

DRUIDS
Celtic priesthood of the later Iron Age, too late to have had a role at Avebury or Stonehenge.

GROOVED WARE
Late neolithic flat based pottery with striped panels, often associated with henges.

HENGE
Circular or oval late neolithic/early Bronze Age ritual earthwork, sometimes with a stone circle.

LONG BARROW
Long neolithic mound which functions as burial place, temple and marker of tribal territory.

MEGALITH
mega = big, lith = stone.

MORTUARY HOUSE
Place safe from scavengers where bodies were defleshed before burial.

NEOLITHIC PERIOD
The New Stone Age from the first settled farmers to the arrival of bronze technology. Dated in Britain to c.4500–2000 BC.

ROUND BARROW
Circular mound covering a prestigious Bronze Age burial.

SARSENS
Natural sandstone blocks found lying on Cretaceous chalk downs and used for megaliths.

SOLSTICE
Longest or shortest day of year.

STONE CIRCLE
Neolithic/Bronze Age ritual arrangement of megaliths, often not circular.

TRILITHON
Three large stones arranged like a doorway of two uprights and a lintel.

WESSEX
The southern English counties of Berkshire, Dorset, Hampshire, Somerset and Wiltshire.

LEFT: *Avebury's Great Circle at dawn.*

BACK COVER: *Avebury.*